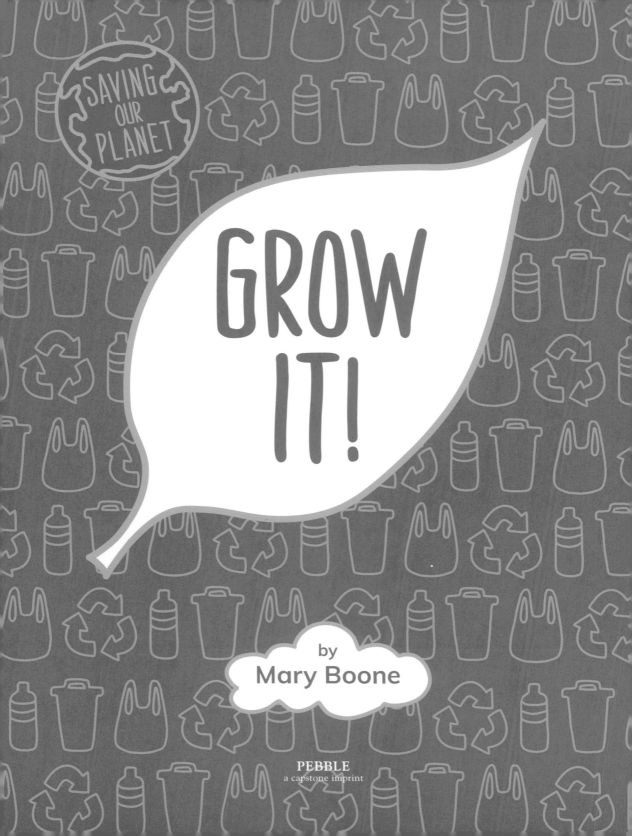

SAVING OUR PLANET

GROW IT!

by **Mary Boone**

PEBBLE
a capstone imprint

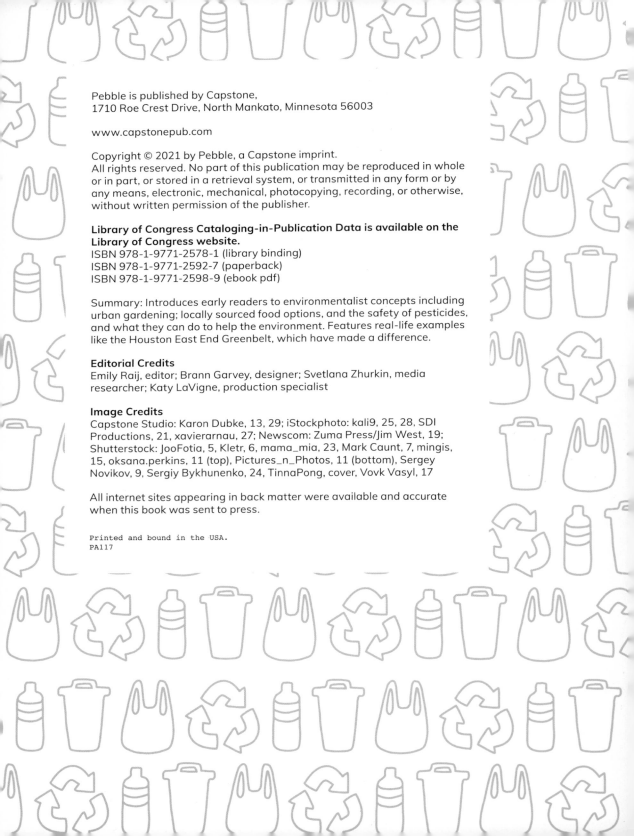

Pebble is published by Capstone,
1710 Roe Crest Drive, North Mankato, Minnesota 56003

www.capstonepub.com

**Library of Congress Cataloging-in-Publication Data is available on the
Library of Congress website.**
ISBN 978-1-9771-2578-1 (library binding)
ISBN 978-1-9771-2592-7 (paperback)
ISBN 978-1-9771-2598-9 (ebook pdf)

Summary: Introduces early readers to environmentalist concepts including
urban gardening; locally sourced food options, and the safety of pesticides,
and what they can do to help the environment. Features real-life examples
like the Houston East End Greenbelt, which have made a difference.

Editorial Credits
Emily Raij, editor; Brann Garvey, designer; Svetlana Zhurkin, media
researcher; Katy LaVigne, production specialist

Image Credits
Capstone Studio: Karon Dubke, 13, 29; iStockphoto: kali9, 25, 28, SDI
Productions, 21, xavierarnau, 27; Newscom: Zuma Press/Jim West, 19;
Shutterstock: JooFotia, 5, Kletr, 6, mama_mia, 23, Mark Caunt, 7, mingis,
15, oksana.perkins, 11 (top), Pictures_n_Photos, 11 (bottom), Sergey
Novikov, 9, Sergiy Bykhunenko, 24, TinnaPong, cover, Vovk Vasyl, 17

All internet sites appearing in back matter were available and accurate
when this book was sent to press.

Printed and bound in the USA.
PA117

TABLE OF CONTENTS

Words in **bold** are in the glossary.

PLANTING FOR THE PLANET

Juicy strawberries. Sweet peas. Crisp green beans. When you plant a garden, you get more than good food. Growing your own food is a great way to help our planet.

That's right. Gardens, trees, bushes, and flowers help keep the earth healthy. They provide food for people and animals. They provide **shelter** for wildlife. Plants can also cool the air around them. They reduce **pollution**. People and animals need plants to live.

Plants provide habitats for wildlife. Many birds rely on trees for their homes. They build nests on branches. Or they may live in holes in tree trunks.

Deer, goats, and rabbits eat leaves off bushes. Fish hide under water lilies. Mice and squirrels use leaves to keep their nests warm. Without plants, many animals would have nowhere to live. They would go hungry.

Plants release oxygen into the air. People and animals breathe in oxygen. They need it to live. But people and animals breathe out **carbon dioxide**. That is a gas plants need to live. Plants pull it from the air through their leaves.

If plants didn't remove carbon dioxide from the air, it would build up. The air would be hard to breathe. Temperatures would rise.

GARDENS DO A LOT OF GOOD

Plants and gardens help the earth in other ways too. Growing your own food cuts down on pollution.

Semitrucks carry food to grocery stores. Many trucks travel thousands of miles. Trucks and other vehicles burn **fuel** that pollutes the air. When food is sent from far away, it needs more packaging. This extra plastic and cardboard makes more trash.

If you have a garden, you might want to **compost**. That is a way of **recycling** natural materials. These include grass clippings, fruit peels, and leftover food. Over time, this waste breaks down. It becomes a rich, dark mix that can be added to soil. Old food helps grow fresh food!

Food scraps and yard waste make up about one-third of what Americans throw away. Composting keeps that out of landfills.

Some people use chemicals to help plants grow. But those fertilizers can be unsafe for people. They can also hurt animals. Rain causes fertilizer to run off gardens. The polluted water flows into drains, rivers, and lakes. It ends up in oceans too. **Algae** grow too fast. Water becomes unhealthy. Fish and other animals die.

Organic fertilizers are better. They are made from natural materials. They help plants grow without chemicals.

GET GROWING AT SCHOOL

Pollination helps gardens grow too. Have you heard the buzz about bees? They move pollen from one plant to another. Many plants need to be pollinated to grow. Apples, cucumbers, blueberries, pumpkins, and strawberries are a few.

Students at Heritage High School in Lynchburg, Virginia, know bees are important. They have a school club called The Pollinators. The club planted trees that attract bees. More bees pollinate more plants.

Without bees, many fruits and vegetables would not grow.

Gardens can help whole neighborhoods. East Houston, Texas, was called a food desert. That means healthy, affordable food was hard to find there. People wanted to fix this problem.

Nearby schools teamed up to grow gardens. Students and teachers planted more than 200 fruit trees. They grew cabbage and potatoes. Now there are 200 community gardens. Each year, East Houston schools give thousands of pounds of fresh vegetables to local food banks.

Many schools have spaces for gardens. Students can plant and care for these gardens. Sometimes gardening is done by an after-school club.

Gardening can be part of class lessons too. Students may measure the size of the garden in math class. They might write about planting in English class. There are many science lessons too. Students may learn about what's living in the soil. Or they may study the life cycle of plants.

SMALL SPACES, COMMUNITY GARDENS, AND FARMERS' MARKETS

People may think they need a big yard to have a garden. But small spaces work too. You can grow vegetables on your deck or balcony. All you need is a container, good soil, and seeds.

If you don't have outdoor space, you can garden inside. Herbs or lettuce will grow in pots on a windowsill. You can even grow bean sprouts inside a jar with no soil at all.

23

Community gardens can be at schools, in front of city buildings, or on empty land. Neighbors or other groups plan and care for these gardens. A garden can bring pollinators to cities. It can provide fresh fruits and vegetables in places without many stores. These gardens bring people together.

Think of neighbors or groups with whom you would like to start a garden. Plan what you will grow and shop for seeds. Set times to work together. Then get gardening!

Can't grow your own food? You can still do your part. Shop at farmers' markets if you can. The food there is locally grown. It comes from small farms near your community. It didn't come from far away on a big truck. That means less pollution and less packaging. And it tastes fresher too.

One garden alone cannot save
the planet. One extra shopper at the
farmers' market cannot end pollution.

But many people doing one helpful thing will add up. Join with your friends and neighbors. Dig. Plant. Weed. Water. And keep thinking about the ways you can help the world.

GLOSSARY

algae (AL-jee)—small plants without roots or stems that grow in water

carbon dioxide (KAHR-buhn dy-AHK-syd)—a gas in the air that people and animals give off and plants use to make food

compost (KOM-pohst)—to mix decaying leaves, vegetables, and other items together so that it can be used to make the soil better for gardening

fuel (FYOOL)—anything that can be burned to give off energy

habitat (HAB-uh-tat)—the natural place and conditions in which a plant or animal lives

organic (or-GAN-ik)—grown using no chemicals or pesticides

oxygen (OK-suh-juhn)—a colorless gas that people and animals breathe

pollination (pol-uh-NAY-shuhn)—to move pollen from plant to plant

pollution (puh-LOO-shuhn)—harmful materials that damage the air, water, and soil

recycle (ree-SYE-kuhl)—the process of using things again instead of throwing them away

READ MORE

Amstutz, Lisa J. *Edible Gardening: Growing Your Own Vegetables, Fruits, and More.* North Mankato, MN: Capstone Press, 2016.

Hillery, Tony, and Jessie Hartland. *Harlem Grown: How One Big Idea Transformed a Neighborhood.* New York: Simon & Schuster Books for Young Readers, 2020.

Raskin, Ben. *Grow: A Family Guide to Growing Fruits and Vegetables.* Boulder, CO: Roost Books, 2017.

INTERNET SITES

Big Green: Video Library
biggreen.org/teaching-in-your-garden/video-library/

Kids Gardening
kidsgardening.org/garden-activities/

My First Garden
web.extension.illinois.edu/firstgarden/

INDEX